I0390998

From
SURVIVAL
To
SIGNIFICANCE

@JEREMYWAITE

• LONDON, England • MMXV

#SignificantBrands

*"Your brand isn't what you say it is,
it's what other people tell their friends it is".*

#SIGNIFICANTBRANDS
~ MANIFESTO ~

1. Significant brands are run by companies who's intentions lie beyond profits. They want to make profits with purpose.
2. Significant brands stand for something larger than themselves and by doing so, they inspire and add value to the lives of everyone they touch.
3. Significant brands understand that customer service is just as important as generating sales, because their most loyal customers are their most valuable asset.
4. Significant brands think big and act small. They believe in the value of knowing each customer by name, no matter how large their customer base is.
5. Significant brands know that they only need to measure a few metrics each day in order to monitor their growth and success. They also understand that just because they have the ability to measure everything, doesn't mean that they should.
6. Significant brands understand that engaging with their fans, followers and subscribers, and building a community, are two totally different things. They prefer the latter knowing that a real community loves, supports and encourages each other. This not only drives sales but accelerates innovation, increases the quality of customer care and provides better insights.
7. Significant brands value employee satisfaction as highly as customer satisfaction.
8. Significant brands communicate with just six objectives, but they execute those objectives with power and precision. They inspire, inform, educate, entertain, challenge people and solve problems.
9. Significant brands appeal to the head *and* the heart.
10. Brands can not become significant on their own, because the true value of a brand lies in what it's customers say to each other, not what the brand says to its audience. Brands are not in control anymore. Its customers are.

A significant brand is a rare breed. Not many of them exist in this world, but when you meet one you soon know about it. Becoming one does not require luck, timing or large advertising budgets. Significant brands simply value their customers more than themselves, and are willing to do the things that other brands don't do.

All Profits From This Book Go To Help Kids Code via
Code.org

Code.org launched in 2013 as a bootstrapped project of co-founders Ali and Hadi Partovi. Their initial work was a video that became #1 on YouTube for a day, and caused 15,000 schools to reach out to them help. Since then, Code.org has expanded to build a full organization supporting a worldwide movement. Their goal is for computer science to be a fixed part of school curriculum. To support that goal, they do work across the education spectrum: designing our own courses or partnering with others, training teachers, partnering with large school districts, helping change government policies, expanding internationally via partnerships, and marketing to break stereotypes.

The vision of code.org is that every student in every school should have the opportunity to learn computer science. They believe that computer science and computer programming should be part of the core curriculum in education, alongside other science, technology, engineering, and mathematics (STEM) courses, such as biology, physics, chemistry and algebra.

- 113,142,155+ kids (48% girls) have tried an hour of code.
- 126,286 teachers have signed up to teach code courses.
- 5,498,861 students are enrolled on coding courses.
- Coding courses are now available in 30+ languages.
- Code.org courses are available in 180 countries.

THE 5 LEVELS OF BRAND LEADERSHIP

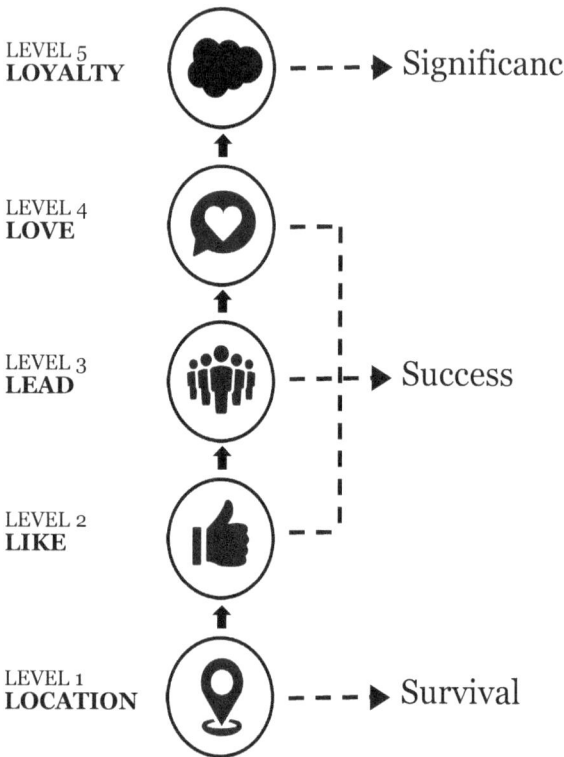

LEVEL 5 **LOYALTY**		Significance
LEVEL 4 **LOVE**		
LEVEL 3 **LEAD**		Success
LEVEL 2 **LIKE**		
LEVEL 1 **LOCATION**		Survival

Every brand has its own story, its own customer journeys and its own culture. That's what makes it special. But different brands exist on different levels because of the *way* that they run their business, and the *way* that they treat their customers during those journeys. Only when we fully understand the challenges that brands face on each level, will we be able to take our own brands from survival to significance.

5 LEVELS OF BRAND LEADERSHIP

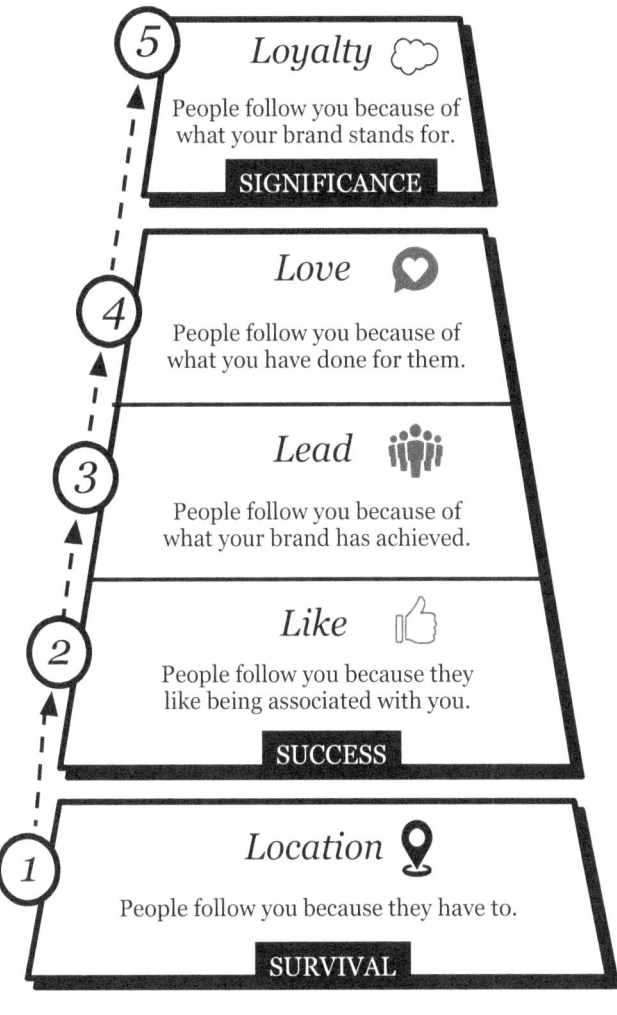

5 Loyalty
People follow you because of what your brand stands for.
SIGNIFICANCE

4 Love
People follow you because of what you have done for them.

3 Lead
People follow you because of what your brand has achieved.

2 Like
People follow you because they like being associated with you.
SUCCESS

1 Location
People follow you because they have to.
SURVIVAL

You can have everything you want in life, if you just help enough other people get what they want.

ZIG ZIGLAR

The World's Greatest Sales Trainer.
(1926 ~ 2012)

Money can't buy you happiness...

But it can buy you a big yacht to pull up right alongside it.

DAVID LEE ROTH

Lead singer of Van Halen inducted into the Rock and Roll Hall of Fame in 2007.

The Norwegian word for sell is selje, which literally means "to serve".

ZIG ZIGLAR

The World's Greatest Sales Trainer.
(1926 ~ 2012)

It's easier than ever to start a company, but harder than ever to build one.

@ALFRED_LIN

Venture Capitalist with Sequoia Capital.

The problem is never the problem. The response to the problem is almost always the problem.

TOM PETERS

Voted one of the world's greatest management consultants and author of Re-imagine.

Your biggest problem is thinking that the current problem you are facing is the problem.

@TONYROBBINS

Author, strategist and speaker. Voted by American Express as one of the world's top 6 business leaders and recognised by Harvard Business Press as one of the world's top 50 business intellectuals.

#SignificantBrands

Leadership is Influence.

JOHN C. MAXWELL

Author and Leadership Coach.
@JohnCMaxwell

People buy into the leader before they buy into the vision.

JOHN C. MAXWELL

Author of The 21 Irrefutable Laws of Leadership and
The world's #1 leadership coach (According to Inc. Magazine)
@JohnCMaxwell

#SignificantBrands

Every business needs a maniac and a minder.

STEPHEN LLOYD

*Lawyer and Social Entrepreneur
(1951-2014)*

Life is short.
Act accordingly.

JACK NICHOLSON

LA Lakers fan. Joker. Storyteller.

It is no longer
survival of the
fittest.

It is survival of the
fastest...

@BRIANSOLIS

Digital Marketing Analyst, Speaker and Author of
"What's the Future of Business?" #WTF

Ideas are a commodity.

Execution of them is not.

@MICHAELDELL

Founder and CEO of Dell inc.
@MichaelDell

First mover advantages are overrated. MySpace was a first mover.

It's better to have an idea best than to have it first.

@JACK

Co-Founder of @Twitter and @Square.

It's more difficult to un-subscribe from a relationship.

DAVID @ARMANO

Global Strategy Director, Edelman Digital
@Armano

If you hate change, you're going to like irrelevance even less.

ERIC SHINSEKI

Former Chief-of-Staff for the US Army and recipient of 3 bronze stars and 2 purple hearts, as a result of his military service in Vietnam

#SignificantBrands

Don't mistake activity for achievement.

COACH JOHN WOODEN

Ex-Head Coach of UCLA Basketball and America's most successful college coach.

It's not enough to do your best. You must know what to do, and **then** do your best.

W. EDWARDS DEMING

Engineer and Management Consultant at Ford Motor Co.
(1900 ~ 1993)

In 1987, Deming was awarded the National Medal of Technology *"For his forceful promotion of statistical methodology, for his contributions to sampling theory, and for his advocacy to corporations and nations of a general management philosophy that has resulted in improved product quality."*

Do what you can.
With what you have.
Where you are.

THEODORE "TEDDY" ROOSEVELT

26th President of the United States.
(1858 ~ 1919)

The only thing worse than starting something and failing...

is not starting something.

SETH GODIN

Author.

It's not necessary to change.

Survival is not mandatory.

W. EDWARDS DEMING

Engineer and Management Consultant at
Ford Motor Co.
(1900 ~ 1993)

Half of my advertising works.

I just don't know which half.*

JOHN WANNAMAKER

Politician, Merchant and Religious Leader.
(1838-1922)

* With so much data at a marketers disposal these days, and the ability
to use predictive analytics and audience insights to understand exactly
what you customer wants and when they want it ~ there is no excuse for
any marketer hiding behind this quote anymore. Just because you might
not know which half works, doesn't mean it's not possible to find out.

Just because you can measure everything doesn't mean that you should.

W. EDWARDS DEMING

Engineer and Management Consultant at Ford Motor Co.
(1900 ~ 1993)

Insights are
things you
don't know,
should know,
but have the
ability to
change.

ERIC SWAYNE

Analyst and Founder of @MutualMind
@ESwayne

Successful brands just do the things that unsuccessful brands are not willing to do.

@JEREMYWAITE

Ex-giraffe keeper, cocktail shaker and strategist @Salesforce.

"*Sir,*" a wealthy man said, when asked how he made his money, "*Sir, I understood my business, and attended to it.*"

I recently discovered an antique book written for Men in Business. It turned out to be worth a great deal as it was a first edition from 1857. In summing up the wisdom from all four volumes, the author said this quote told business men everything they needed to know about growing their business. Not bad advice ~ especially considering it is 157 years old.

Everybody says social media is some kind of unicorn.

But maybe it's just a horse.

@JAYBAER

Social Media Strategist and Author.

Whenever you find yourself on the side of the majority, it is time to pause and reflect.

MARK TWAIN

Storyteller.
(1835-1910)

Better to have 100 people love you than 1 million people kinda like you.

BRIAN CHESKY

Co-Founder and CEO Airbnb
@Bchesky

It took Hilton Hotels 93 years to build an inventory of 600,000 rooms. It took Airbnb 4 years. Asked how he launched so successfully, Brian said that he didn't. When Airbnb first launched nobody noticed, so Brian launched 3 times until people did notice!

#SignificantBrands

The best minds of my generation are thinking about how to make people click ads.

That sucks.

JEFF HAMMERBACHER

Co-Founder of Cloudera and Facebook's First Data Scientist

He now works at Mt. Sinai Medical School teaching physicians and medical researches how to use big data to solve many of the world's greatest medical challenges.

Passion is a *verb* not a *noun*.

@JOHNCMAXWELL

Leadership Coach and Best Selling Author.

#SignificantBrands

Marketing is no longer about the stuff you make but the stories you tell.

SETH GODIN

Author.

Established in 1910 used to be an asset.
These days it feels like a liability.

SETH GODIN

Author.

Whoever tells the best stories goes home with the most marbles.

@JEREMYWAITE

Lover of Purpose Driven Brands.

Time you enjoy wasting is not wasted time.

JOHN LENNON

Singer song writer.
(1940-1980)

Business has only two functions; marketing and innovation.

PETER DRUCKER

*Management Consultant and winner of
the Presidential Medal of Freedom.
(1909-2005)*

Culture eats strategy for breakfast.

PETER DRUCKER

Management Consultant and winner of the Presidential Medal of Freedom.
(1909-2005)

If we can keep our competitors focused on us while we stay focused on the customer, ultimately we'll turn out all right.

JEFF BEZOS

Amazon CEO.

Try not to become a man of success.

But a man of value.

ALBERT EINSTEIN

Theoretical Physicist
(1903 ~ 1919)

If you are bored with social media, it is most likely that you are trying to get more value from it, than you are creating for your customers.

@FastCompany

#SignificantBrands

Successful managers know what they are good at.

Successful leaders know what their people are good at.

JOHN C. MAXWELL

Author and Leadership Coach
@JohnCMaxwell

#SignificantBrands

You can't manage what you don't measure.

W. EDWARDS DEMING

Engineer, Statistician and Management Consultant.
(1900 ~ 1993)

It's not enough to do your best, you must know what to do and then do your best.

W. EDWARDS DEMING

Engineer, Statistician and Management Consultant.
(1900 ~ 1993)

I'm more proud of the things we didn't do, than I am of what we did.

Steve Jobs on why it's not important to do everything. When Steve rejoined Apple as interim-CEO in 1997 the first thing he did was simplify everything. He cut down Apples product list from over 30 lines to just 4 core products.

Marketers should be similarly proud of what they don't measure (providing they are measuring the right things in the first place, obviously).

http://www.slideshare.net/jeremywaite/the-worlds-most-valuable-whiteboard-session-by-steve-jobs

Established in 1912 used to be an asset. These days it feels like a liability.

SETH GODIN

Author, TED Speaker and Marketing Genius.

Concentrate your energy, your thoughts and your capital.

The way to become rich is to put all your eggs into one basket and then watch that basket.

ANDREW CARNEGIE

Businessman and Philanthropist.
(1835-1919)

The formula two and two make five is not without its attractions.

FYODOR DOSTOYEVSKY

Russian Novelist, Journalist & Philosopher.
(1821-1881)

In God we trust.

All others must
bring data.

W. EDWARDS DEMING

Data Scientist and Statistician
(1900-1993)

*If we have data,
let's look at
data.*

*If all we have
are opinions,
let's go with
mine.*

JIM BARKSDALE

Ex-CEO Netscape.

The most exciting phrase to hear in science, the one that heralds new discoveries, is not "Eureka!" but rather "Hmm... that's funny..."

ISAAC ASIMOV

Russian science fiction author / editor of over 500 books including I-Robot and Professor of Biochemistry at Columbia University.

We ask too much of technology and not enough of ourselves.

@NATESILVER538

Statistician, founder and editor-in-chief of Fivethirtyeight.
The world's most respected data journalism site.

Any sufficiently advanced technology is indistinguishable from magic.

ARTHUR C. CLARKE

Inventor, Author and Co-writer of 2001 : A Space Odyssey.
(1917-2008)

However beautiful the strategy, we should occasionally look at the results.

Sir WINSTON CHURCHILL

Former Prime Minster of United Kingdom.
(1874-1965)

Caring about your customers is the right thing to do. It makes for a better company, a better society, and a better life.

FRED REICHHELD

Bain & Co and Co-Creator of the NPS Score.

All business operations can be reduced to three words: people, product and profits.

Unless you've got a good team, you can't do much with the other two.

LEE IACOCCA

Former Chairman of Ford and President and CEO of Chrysler.

Technology is nothing. What's important is that you have faith in people, that they're basically good and smart, and if you give them tools, they'll do wonderful things with them.

STEVE JOBS

*Apple Co-Founder and Ex-CEO Pixar
(1955-2011)*

Your most unhappy customers are your greatest source of learning.

@BILLGATES

Philanthropist & Co-Founder of Microsoft.

Customer service is one of the only times that you have 100% of your customers attention.

@TEDRUBIN

The World's "Most Connected" CMO.
#RonR

Most people over estimate what they can do in a year and under estimate what they can do in ten years.

@BILLGATES

Philanthropist & Co-Founder of Microsoft.

"If it ain't broke don't fix it" doesn't apply anymore ~ because if it ain't broke, it's probably obsolete.

@BILLGATES

Philanthropist & Co-Founder of Microsoft.

Poor people have big TVs.

Rich people have big libraries.

JIM ROHN

Author of "The Art of Exceptional Living", alongside many other timeless books well worth reading.
(1930-2009)

Success isn't the same as talent.

The world is full of incredibly talented people who never succeed at anything.

TIM GROVER

Performance Coach and Personal Trainer to NBA Champions Michael Jordan, Dwayne Wade and Kobe Bryant.

Make it simple.
But significant.

DON DRAPER

Founding Partner,
Sterling Cooper Draper Pryce.

I'm here to build something for the long term.

Anything else is a distraction.

MARK ZUCKERBERG

Co-founder Facebook.com
Facebook.com/Zuck   @Finkd

Keep your minimum wage employees happy, and your customers will be happy ~ and then your investors will be happy.

SAM WALTON

Founder of @Walmart in 1962 with one store in Arkansas. Walmart is now the largest grocery chain in the world, generating over $447 Billion in sales from 10,000 stores with a brand valued at $46.7Bn. Walmart now use the vast majority of their profits to educate school children about healthy living through their foundation.

You can't purchase loyalty.

President FRANK UNDERWOOD

@HouseofCards

We must create more value than we capture.

TIM O'REILLY

Technology Curator and Publisher of Dummies Guide Books.

How do we make the economy work better?

@JACK DORSEY

Co-Founder of two billion dollar startups ~
@Square and @Twitter.

Marketing used to be about creating a myth and selling it; Now it's about finding a truth and sharing it.

MARC MATHIEU

SVP Marketing at Unilever

Great social entrepreneurs are natural tellers of stories, many of which are true.

Professor MUHAMMAD YUNUS

Social Entrepreneur and Nobel Laureate

Social media has more to do with sociology and psychology than technology.

@BRIANSOLIS

Author, Speaker and Principal at Altimeter Group.

*Engaging with your fans and building a community are two **totally** different things.*

@MITCHJOEL

Author, Podcaster and President of Twist Image.

#SignificantBrands

The difference between an audience and a community is which way the chairs are facing.

@CHRIS BROGAN

Author, Journalist and Marketing Consultant.

Unless we stand for something, we shall fall for anything.

Rev. PETER MARSHALL

U.S. Senate Chaplain
(1902 ~ 1949)

We don't need new technology, we need better business models.

JEROEN TAS

CIO @Philips and one of the most inspirational technology visionaries I've ever met. He's driving Philips towards their goal of improving the lives of 3 billion people by 2025.

It's not what you make, it's what you stand for.

JAMES COLLINS

Author of "Good to Great".

CEOs used to be judged by how well they acted in a crisis.

Now they are judged by how well they anticipate one.

WADAR KHANFAR

Al Jazeera, Director General (2003-2011)

If you give $1 you are a philanthropist.

@CHARLESBEST

CEO, Co-Founder of Donors Choose.

Companies are no longer competing against each other, they are competing against speed.

MARC @BENIOFF

Co-Founder of Salesforce.com, American Entrepreneur and Philanthropist.

Quality means doing it right when no one is looking.

HENRY FORD

Industrialist, Philanthropist and founder of Ford Motor Co. (1888 – 1947)

The competitor to be feared is one who never bothers about you at all, but goes on making his own business better all the time.

HENRY FORD

Industrialist, Philanthropist and founder of Ford Motor Co. (1888 – 1947)

The man who stops advertising to save money is the like the man who stops the clock to save time.

HENRY FORD

Industrialist, Philanthropist and founder of Ford Motor Co. (1888 – 1947)

*I have not failed.
I've just found
10,000 ways
that don't work.*

THOMAS EDISON

Industrialist, Inventor and Co-Founder of General Electric, on the
process of inventing the world's first practical incandescent light
bulb.

(1847 – 1931)

Each of us has a capacity to make business not only a source of economic wealth, but also a force for social and economic justice.

WALTER HAAS Jr.

Levi Strauss & Co. CEO 1958-1970

We are not so much retailers with a mission as missionaries who retail.

WALTER ROBB

Co-CEO Wholefoods Market.

*We believe that you
make your mark
in the world not just
by what you do,
but also how you do it.*

LEVI STRAUS

Founder of Levi Strauss & Co.
(1829-1902)

If you organize your life around your passion, you can turn your passion into your story and then turn your story into something bigger ~ something that matters.

@BLAKEMYCOSKIE

Founder @TOMS and One of My Favourite People in the World.

I believe what we're doing is affecting the way businesses will be built for hundreds of years to come.

Stay true to what you believe, and what your message is, and then let the chips fall where they fall..

@BLAKEMYCOSKIE

Founder @TOMS

Businesses need profits to survive. The less we make, the less we will have to give away, and the less other companies will think we have a mission that is worth imitating.

YVON CHOUINARD

Climber, Founder of Patagonia and Philanthropist.
@PATAGONIA

Invention is going from zero to one.

Innovation is going from zero to one thousand.

YVON CHOUINARD

Climber, Founder of Patagonia and Philanthropist.
@PATAGONIA

Note to brands:

If you don't have a cause, get one.

ARIANNA HUFFINGTON

Founder of Huffington Post
@ARIANNAHUFF

There is a difference between offering a service and being willing to serve.

They both include giving, but only one is generous.

@SIMONSINEK

*Author, Speaker
and Cultural Anthropologist*

People don't buy what you do, they buy why you do it.

@SIMONSINEK

Author, Speaker and Cultural Anthropologist

A product can be quite sterile until you give it a context and an environment.

That's what's important about digital, its allowed all of us to tell stories.

CHRISTOPHER BAILEY

Burberry Chief Creative Officer and CEO

Timing, perseverance and ten years of trying will eventually make you look like an overnight success.

@BIZ STONE

Co-Founder @Twitter and Jelly.

The real purpose of running isn't to win, it's to test the limits of the human heart.

BILL BOWERMAN

Co-Founder of Nike and inventor of the waffle sole. (1936-1999)

At Cadbury we live out our values in the same way we do business.

That was true yesterday. It is true today. It will be true tomorrow.

TODD STITZER

Cadbury CEO 2003-2010

A brand with nothing behind it is a pretty hollow thing.

Sir ANTHONY BAMFORD

Chairman JCB

Machines should be nothing more than tools for extending the powers of the human beings who use them.

THOMAS WATSON Jnr.

Ex-President of IBM (1952-1971) and recipient of the Presidential Medal of Freedom. Labeled "The greatest capitalist in history", he was named one of the most influential people of the 20th century by TIME magazine.

He who dies with the least toys wins.

Because the more you know, the less you need.

YVON CHOUINARD

Climber, Founder of Patagonia and Philanthropist.
@PATAGONIA

I've heard there's going to be a recession.

I've decided not to participate.

WALTER ELIAS "WALT" DISNEY

Cartoonist, Animator, Film Producer and Entrepreneur (1901-1966)

*Disney employees attempted to keep Walt's spirit alive by constantly asking themselves, "**What would Walt do?**". Perhaps they thought that if they asked that question, they would come up with something original that would remain true to Walt's pioneering spirit.*

In fact this kind of thinking only accomplished the opposite. Because it looked backwards and not forward, it tethered the place to the status quo.

@EDCATMULL

President of Pixar and Disney Animation Studios. Ed grew up in the 1950's inspired by the two most influential people of his day. Ed says that Albert Einstein inspired his head and Walt Disney inspired his heart.

"You can't manage what you can't measure" is a maxim that is taught and believed by many in both the business and education sectors. But in fact, the phrase is ridiculous ~ something said by people who are unaware of how much is hidden.

A large portion of what we manage can't be measured, and not realising this has unintended consequences".

@EDCATMULL

Author of Creativity Inc. One of the best books on Creativity and the power of ideas that I've ever read.

#SignificantBrands

Ideas people start their day looking for trouble.

WALTER ELIAS "WALT" DISNEY

*Cartoonist, Animator, Film Producer and Entrepreneur
(1901-1966)*

Strong men know when to compromise and that all principles can be compromised to serve a greater purpose.

ANDREW CARNEGIE

Businessman and Philanthropist and a believer that speed is one of the biggest enemies of success, regularly telling his managers, " The first one gets the oyster. The second gets the shell". (Survival of the fastest isn't a 20th century concept). (1835-1919)

I'm a man who thinks the best is always yet to come.

PRESIDENT JOSÉ MUJICA

President of Uruguay. He gave away 90% of his $12,000 salary to charity and drives a 1987 VW Beetle. He lives in a one bedroom farmhouse with his three legged dog called Manuela, and despite being known as the world's poorest president, he has never seen himself as poor.

If what you have done yesterday still looks big to you, you haven't done much today.

COACH MIKE KRZYZEWSKI

NCAA Basketball Coach of Duke. One of the most successful coaches of all time. Five NCAA championships, 12 conference titles and an all-time NCAA winning percentage of 76.7% (1018-310).

Now is the time for giving back?

If you're giving back you took too much.

RICARDO SEMLER

CEO of SEMCO Partners. Re-invented industrial democracy and corporate engineering. His CFO predicted he could have made 4.1X more money it he saved it up to give away later, but he decided to give it away each day instead.

The older I get the less I listen to what people say and the more I look at what they do.

ANDREW CARNEGIE

Businessman and Philanthropist.
(1835-1919)

Purpose is something we can never take for granted; the moment we do, it starts to be forgotten and soon disappears.

JOHN MACKEY

Co-Founder @WHOLEFOODS Market and Author of Conscious Capitalism

#SignificantBrands

There's more to life than increasing it's speed.

MAHATMA GANDHI

Peaceful Protester and Champion of Indian Independence. (1883-1944)

Let's go invent tomorrow instead of worrying about what happened yesterday.

STEVE JOBS

American Entrepreneur, Marketer, Founder, Inventor.
(1955-2011)

Never doubt that a small group of thoughtful, committed citizens can change the world; indeed, it's the only thing that ever has.

MARGARET MEAD

Author, Speaker and Cultural Anthropologist (1901-1978)

Read

Purpose + Profit ~ Arianna Huffington's blog
Conscious Capitalism by John Mackey
Mission by Michael Hayman & Nick Giles
How to Win Friends and Influence People by Dale Carnegie
Re-Imagine by Tom Peters
Everything written by Seth Godin
What's the Future of Business by Brian Solis
Lovemarks by Kevin Roberts
Innovators by Walter Isaacson
Greatest Business Decisions of All Time by Forbes
Outliers by Malcolm Gladwell
Good Strategy Bad Strategy by Richard Rumelt
The Social Organisation by Gartner
The Ultimate Question 2.0 by Fred Reichheld
Loyalty Effect by Fred Reichheld
The Purpose Driven Life by Rick Warren
Today Matters by John Maxwell
Money: Master the Game by Tony Robbins
Behind the Cloud by Marc Benioff
Things a Little Bird Told Me by Biz Stone
Creativity, Inc by Ed Catmull
Big Bang Disruption by Larry Downes & Paul Nunes
Give and Take by Adam Grant
Bold by Shaun Smith & Andy Milligan
Give Smart by Thomas Tierney & Joel Fleishman
Signal and the Noise by Nate Silver
You Only Have to Be Right Once by Randall Lane
It's Not What You Stand For by Roy Spence
Zero to One by Peter Thiel
Great by Choice by Jim Collins
Relentless by Tim Grover
How Many Friends Does One Person Need? by Robin Dunbar
Flip the Funnel by Joseph Jaffe
CTRL ALT Delete by Mitch Joel
Lean In by Sheryl Sandberg
Whatever You Think Think the Opposite by Paul Arden
Wizard of Menlo Park by Randall Stross

Watch

Need more inspiration? Search YouTube for videos;

Steve Jobs ~ Marketing Strategy (Crazy Ones)

Simon Sinek ~ Start with Why (TED)

Seth Godin Inbound 2013

Gary Vaynerchuk Inc 500

Susan Etlinger ~ What do we do with all this big data?

Jack Dorsey ~ Curiosity & Inspiration (Stanford)

John Maxwell ~ 5 Levels of Leadership

Rick Warren ~ A Life of Purpose (TED)

W. Edwards Deming ~ The 14 Points

Robin Dunbar ~ 150 Friends

Bill Gates & Steve Jobs ~ D5 Conference 2007

Henry Ford ~ Model T Documentary

Chip Kidd ~ Designing Books is No Laughing Matter

Simon Sinek and Summer Rain ~ SRO Conversations #22

Nate Silver ~ Art & Science of Prediction at LSE

Scott Galloway ~ Four Horsemen

All the Studio 1.0 Interview on Bloomberg West

Steve Jobs ~ iPhone launch 2007

Chip Conley ~ Measuring What Makes Life Worthwhile

Master of the Universe (Documentary)

Terms & Conditions May Apply (Documentary)

ENRON ~ Smartest Guys in the Room (Documentary)

Tony Robbins ~ Why We Do What We Do

New York Times: Page One

The Internet's Own Boy

Wikileaks ~ We Steal Secrets

Ricardo Semler ~ Radical Wisdom for a Company (TED)

Sir Tim Berners-Lee ~ LeWeb 2014

Mad Men Season 1 ~ Kodak Carousel Pitch

Mark Zuckerberg ~ Tsinhua University 2014

Richard Rumelt ~ Good Strategy Bad Strategy (LSE)

Charlie Rose Interview with Larry Page

Foundation Interview's with Kevin Rose

Any talks by Yvon Chouinard

Follow

Everyone is different and each of us have different people who flick our switches. If you're interested in the stuff I talk about, feel free to follow me on Twitter @JeremyWaite or have a look at who I follow. Looking at everyone that your favourite publication or organisation follows is always a good idea too.

Some of my favourite news sources include:

- Fast Company
- Forbes
- Fortune
- Bloomberg West
- Business Week
- Conscious Capitalism
- Adbusters
- Monocle Magazine
- Tech Crunch
- Venture Beat
- The Next Web
- Mashable
- Seeking Alpha
- Gartner Inc.
- Forrester Research
- Comscore
- Harvard Business Review
- FT.com
- Marketing Week
- Brand Republic
- The Drum
- FiveThirtyEight.com
- Hacker News

Best piece of advice I ever received about who to follow? **Just follow everyone @ElonMusk is following.** (The same can be said of @codeorg).

@JeremyWaite

Jeremy Waite is a strategist and evangelist for Salesforce.com, based in London. Born in Manchester, his career started in the family printing business before setting up his own brand consultancy, working for some of the world's largest brands. From Survival to Significance is Jeremy's second book after writing "Sex, Brands & Rock'n'Roll" in 2010.

Jeremy has worked with Twitter, Facebook, Google and Adobe before he landed at Salesforce, where he now spends most of his time talking to executives about digital transformation, how to build a customer company and philanthropy.

He loves whiskey, cycling and collecting rare business books. You can chat to him on twitter @JeremyWaite where you can ask him if he really did once work as a giraffe keeper.

www.ingramcontent.com/pod-product-compliance
Lightning Source LLC
Chambersburg PA
CBHW072211170526
45158CB00002BA/552